THE EDWARD DOUGLASS WHITE
LECTURES ON CITIZENSHIP

Previous Edward Douglass White Lectures

1934   New Frontiers of Citizenship
        Howard W. Odum, University of North Carolina
1935   Three Pacts of Peace
        Manley O. Hudson, Harvard University
1936   The Future of the Constitution
        William Yandell Eliott, Harvard University
1937   Some Ways of a Written Constitution
        Thomas Reed Powell, Harvard University
1938   The State in the Twentieth Century
        Herman Finer, London School of Economics
1939   The New Leviathan   The State in Crisis
        Robert Morrison MacIver, Columbia University
1940   Some Problems of Freedom and Democracy in the New World
        Frank Porter Graham, University of North Carolina
1941   Citizenship and Education
        Robert M. Hutchins, University of Chicago
1943   Total War and the Constitution
        Edward S. Corwin, Princeton University
1948   The President and the Congress
        Conflict, Compromise and Cooperation
        Louis Brownlow, University of Chicago
1950   Morality and Administration
        Paul H. Appleby, Syracuse University
1952   Private Groups and Democratic Government
        *William Willard Wirtz, Northwestern University School of
        Law*
1953   The States and the Nation
        Leonard D. White, University of Chicago
1954   A Larger Concept of Community
        *Jefferson B. Fordham, University of Pennsylvania Law
        School*
1955   The Political Background of the Federal Convention
        William W. Crosskey, University of Chicago Law School
1956   Freedom and Administrative Restraints
        Walter Gellhorn, Columbia University Law School
1957   The Supreme Court in Retreat, 1920–1946
        Alpheus T. Mason, Princeton University
1958   Freedom and the Nature of Man
        Lon L. Fuller, Harvard University
1959   The American Tradition of Equality
        Robert J. Harris, Vanderbilt University
1960   World Rule of Law
        Arthur Larson, Duke University

The Cold War:
Retrospect and Prospect

FREDERICK L. SCHUMAN

The Cold War:

LOUISIANA STATE

Retrospect

and Prospect

UNIVERSITY PRESS

Other Books by Frederick L. Schuman

American Policy Toward Russia Since 1917, *1928*
War and Diplomacy in the French Republic, *1931*
International Politics, *1st ed., 1933; 6th ed., 1958*
Rotary, *1934*
The Conduct of German Foreign Policy, *1934*
The Nazi Dictatorship, *1st ed., 1935; 2d ed., 1936*
Germany Since 1918, *1937*
Europe on the Eve, *1939*
Night Over Europe, *1941*
Design for Power (*with George Brodsky*), *1942*
Soviet Politics at Home and Abroad, *1946*
The Commonwealth of Man, *1952*
Russia Since 1917, *1957*
Government in the Soviet Union, *1961*

Copyright 1962 by
Louisiana State University Press
Library of Congress Catalog Card Number: 62–16466
Manufactured in the United States of America by
Kingsport Press, Inc.
Designed by Ernst A. Seemann

TO MY SOUTHERN COUSIN

Dorothy Schulze Stafford

WITH RESPECT, GRATITUDE
AND AFFECTION

Preface

LECTURES SHOULD BE PREPARED FOR ORAL DELIV-
ery to a visible and immediate audience. Articles
and books should be styled for perusal by invisible
and remote readers. These sound precepts of
craftsmanship in the arts of communication are
here, in some measure, violated. A few prelimi-
nary words of explanation are thus in order.

What follows in these pages is the verbatim text, as taped, transcribed, and only slightly "edited," of three addresses given at Louisiana State University, March 27, 28, and 29, 1961, in the series (of which this is the twenty-first) of the "Edward Douglass White Lectures on Citizenship," jointly sponsored by the Department of Government, the Law School, and the Graduate School of LSU. Most of the preceding lectures have dealt with American constitutional law. Many have been amplified into full-length books, with appropriate documentation. The results have been admirable. In the present case my kindly hosts in Baton Rouge suggested three lectures on the Soviet Union, to which proposal I cheerfully assented—the more readily because I have been puzzling over the USSR for more than thirty years (with inconclusive conclusions), while American constitutional law has been, for me, a peripheral concern and is in any case a painful subject in the Old South in mid-century.

I am deeply grateful to LSU collectively—and to the Graduate School, the Law School, and the Department of Government individually—for the opportunity of public expression here reproduced in print. I am particularly indebted to Professor

René de Visme Williamson, Dean Paul M. Hebert, Librarian Sidney Smith, and Donald R. Ellegood, director of the LSU Press, along with many other good people in Baton Rouge, for their helpfulness and warm hospitality. Needless to say, none of those here named or left nameless is in any way responsible for any errors of fact or judgment in the pages which follow.

Baton Rouge in March, and doubtless at other seasons, is a paradise of birds and flowers which can be appreciated only by those who have experienced it. Louisiana, where my mother was born, offers to visitors many rare gifts: heartfelt welcome, superb *cuisine,* and exquisitely beautiful landscapes and gardens which have few parallels elsewhere. All of this, I know full well, may be deemed to have nothing to do with the subject matter of these lectures, any more than the obvious anguish of spirit induced among my hosts (for various and often conflicting motivations) by federal efforts to promote racial desegregation. All such considerations may be dismissed as irrelevant to the content of the lectures which follow by all whose minds are "compartmentalized." But I believe that all these matters are related in a world in which Russians and Americans and many other peoples are earnestly concerned with aesthetics and cooking and all the tangled problems of relations among people of divergent racial or national backgrounds.

To pursue these reflections would be unseemly. The lectures which appear herewith are commentaries on a remote and alien (or "enemy") human community on the opposite side of the globe. For better or worse, these words of wisdom or folly have not been amplified and footnoted into a lengthy tome, with references and illustrations, but are here presented as they were delivered, in the hope and expectation that such a presentation may possibly contribute more effectively to human survival in the thermonuclear age than a detailed, dull, and documented study. The reader will decide whether this anticipation is in any way justified.

I have chosen to add to the text of the lectures a short and selected bibliography of forty-two titles which some readers, seriously concerned with the subject, may find useful in the further pursuit of their inquiries. May they look for light and find it, amid the murk and gloom of anti-Soviet and pro-Soviet literature—both available in such abundance in contemporary America as to benumb the mind.

Again my thanks to my gracious hosts in Baton Rouge; my profound appreciation for their aid in making possible this publication; and my continuing hope that all of us together may find the road to life and to creative competition in contributing toward the health, wealth, and happiness of mankind.

FREDERICK L. SCHUMAN

June 1, 1961
Williamstown, Mass.

Postscript (Spring, 1962): These lectures were originally delivered under the title of "The Soviet Union: Retrospect and Prospect." The present title appears more appropriate in view of subsequent events and in consideration of the circumstance that the lectures are more concerned with East-West relations than with domestic developments in the USSR. Readers who desire a detailed and documented account of these matters should read D. F. Fleming's *The Cold War and Its Origins* (Vol. I, 1917–50; Vol. II, 1950–60; 1158 pages), published in the spring of 1961 by George Allen and Unwin of London and in the autumn of 1961 by Doubleday of New York. This monumental and definitive work —much neglected thus far because its interpretations of the record (like my own) do not conform to prevailing American stereotypes—will long remain, in my judgment, the best account in print of the follies and frustrations in which Americans and Russians alike have involved themselves since alliance gave way to animosity after World War II.

As for the rest, the words and deeds of decision-makers on both sides since March of 1961 have, it seems to me, confirmed the analyses offered in the following pages. The third Program of the CPSU, adopted at Party Congress XXII in October, 1961, spells out the new vision of a communist society as imagined by the Marxist masters of Muscovy. President Kennedy's resolves in the summer of 1961, amid the synthetic Berlin "war crisis," to increase arms spending, call up reserves, and inaugurate a nation-wide network of "fall-out shelters" in preparation for thermonuclear combat, exemplified anew the American delusion that the Communist challenge is a military challenge to be met by military means. The same delusion found new expression in American intervention in South

Vietnam in 1961–1962. Since the challenge is of a wholly different character, it must be met by wholly different means. If different means prove politically possible, the future we face may not be one of atomic coannihilation but one of bright promise for better days to come.

F. L. S.

Contents

Preface   **ix**

Lecture One   The Third Rome   3

Lecture Two   The Social Order   33

Lecture Three   Beyond the Cold War   69

Selected Bibliography   101

The Cold War:
Retrospect and Prospect

Lecture One

The Third Rome

THE PROBLEMS OF HUMAN RELATIONS, ABOUT which I have been asked to speak in this series of Edward Douglass White lectures, are difficult and dark and dismal. In many respects they are dangerous and indeed potentially disastrous for us and for all mankind. After many years of travel and study and writing about these problems, I must admit with the meager wisdom of experience and with the modesty of middle age that I feel no confidence that I can make a constructive contribution to their hopeful resolution. Yet we are all in honor bound to make the best of our opportunities, even as we take cognizance of our difficulties.

We are met together in what the Russians have long called a "Time of Trouble." We have troubles —most difficult and dangerous troubles—throughout the world, some, though by no means all, of which stem from the frightening fact that one-third of mankind under Russian leadership and another one-third of mankind under American leadership have both been busily engaged for a good many years in preparing to wage war against one another. These troubles I propose to discuss, for this is an issue of life or death for all Americans and all Russians and many other peoples. War, as old as human civilization, has never posed such a fateful and fatal issue in all the human past.

When, one hundred years ago, your ancestors and my ancestors in South and North alike resorted to war to resolve their differences in the military conflict we are now engaged in commemorating, known in the North as the "Civil War" or the "War of the Rebellion" and in the South as the "War Between the States" or the "War for Southern Independence," no one assumed on either side that the result, whatever it might be, would be the total destruction of civilization. Today, in the age of H-bombs and intercontinental ballistic missiles with thermonuclear warheads, we are obliged to assume, if we are realists, that war between America and Russia would mean the destruction of civilization. General John Medaris of the United States Air Force estimated a year ago that the destructive power of the American stockpile of atomic and thermonuclear weapons was equivalent to ten tons of TNT for every man, woman, and child now living on the face of the earth. Other reliable estimates would indicate that the United States has a theoretical thermonuclear capacity for killing the entire population of the Soviet Union twenty-five times over and that the Soviet Union has a theoretical thermonuclear capacity for killing the entire population of the United States ten times over. Therefore, a continuation of the arms race and continued preparations for war in the 1960's, unlike the decisions of Americans, North and South, in the 1860's, constitute not a rational reliance on force in pursuit of political purposes, but an irrational and quite insane formula for the probable suicide of the human race.

These lectures will be frankly devoted to exploring the possibilities and prospects of peace between America and Russia on the assumption that war between America and Russia would mean mutual coannihilation. Let me begin with a historical survey of Russian attitudes and policies toward the non-Russian world, on the premise that such a survey may throw some light on present trends and future prospects in Russian attitudes and policies toward the non-Russian world. Our initial questions are these: How do the rulers of Russia behave toward the West and why do they behave the way they behave? A corollary question is: How may we expect them to behave in the future in the light of the long past and in the light of the triumphs, the tragedies, and the immense transformations of the past forty-five years? These questions have long been regarded in the West as unanswerable and insoluble.

In addressing the House of Commons on October 1, 1939, Winston Churchill used a phrase which has since been quoted thousands of times. He said: "I cannot forecast to you the action of Russia. It is a riddle wrapped in a mystery inside an enigma." Perhaps so, or perhaps no. I shall make no pretense of disposing of the enigma or solving the mystery or answering the riddle, but I would like to submit for your critical consideration some possible clues which may promote comprehension and understanding. Winston Churchill himself, in the less quoted statements which followed those I have just given, said: "But perhaps there is a key. That key is Russian national interest."

We are concerned here with the behavior and misbehavior—past, present, and future, insofar as we can foresee the future—of the Marxist rulers of Muscovy in dealing with the non-Marxist and non-Muscovite world. Many simple explanations of this behavior or misbehavior are available, ranging from total depravity and original sin to totalitarian despotism, World Revolution, capitalist villainy, Pan-Slavic imperialism, the Russian soul, and Wall Street plots. Each of these explanations appears to afford adequate emotional satisfaction to those accepting it. To offer another and more complex interpretation may therefore be something of a disservice; yet a reconsideration of the problem may be in order and may not be entirely fruitless. My purpose will be explanation and analysis, not advocacy nor defense. What will be said here will represent entirely a personal view, not that of any political party, or faction, or group; not that of any government agency or branch of public service, civil or military, state or federal; and not that of Williams College or Louisiana State University. Any resemblance between this view and any other view, living or dead, will be purely coincidental.

What many of us find most baffling in our contemplation of Russian attitudes and policies toward the outer world is a persistent and striking ambiguity or dualism or ambivalence which makes it difficult for us to decide whether the power-holders in the Kremlin are responsible rulers of a sovereign state or are fanatical disciples of a cult of revolutionary subversion and messianic universalism. The fact, of course, is that they are both and are therefore victims of a peculiar kind of political double-headedness which gives rise to grave difficulties for themselves and for others.

Perhaps there is symbolic significance in the fact that the early Dukes of Muscovy borrowed the double-headed eagle of Byzantium as their emblem of power. Yet this dualism of roles, this confrontation and contradiction of political purposes, to which I here seek to call attention, is not unique or unprecedented in the experience of past civilizations. A comparable double-headedness or dualism of roles is to be found in the twin functions, secular and religious, of the Caesars of ancient Rome; of the sovereign pontiffs of the Catholic Church and the Papal States; of the caliphs of Islam; the Holy Roman emperors; the great Mongol khans; some of the leaders of the Protestant Reformation; certainly the French Jacobins; and the spokesmen of those simultaneously national and universal aspirations symbolized by the names of Thomas Jefferson, Woodrow Wilson, and Franklin D. Roosevelt. In short, it has happened before and it will doubtless happen again —wholly apart from Marxism, Leninism, and Stalinism—that secular potentates of temporal and local realms, dealing with other sovereigns in State Systems comprising many sovereignties, are also spiritual and ideological high priests of timeless and universal cults whose converts aim at worldwide conversion, subversion, revolution, or salvation. We are not unfamiliar with this phenomenon in our own relatively brief American experience. In Russian experience this phenomenon is at least as old as the Khanate of the Golden Horde, indeed as old as Byzantium from which Russia derived its Christianity and its earliest visions of universal empire.

As early as the year 1505, fifty-two years after the fall of Byzantium to the Ottoman Turks, the Abbot Philotheus of Pskov monastery wrote the following greeting to Basil III, son of Ivan the Great and father of Ivan the Terrible, Duke of Muscovy, and Autocrat of all the Russias:

> The church of ancient Rome fell because of the Apollinarian heresy. As to the second Rome, the church of Constantinople, it has been hewn by the axes of Ishmaelites. But this third new Rome, the Holy Apostolic Church under thy mighty rule, shines throughout the entire world more brightly than the sun. All the Orthodox Christian realms have converged in thine own. Thou are the sole Autocrat of the universe, the only Caesar of the Christians. Two Romes have fallen, but the third stands and no fourth can ever be.

Almost four hundred years later, in the year 1880, but still a whole generation before the great revolution, Fyodor Dostoievsky, speaking at the dedication of the Pushkin monument in Moscow, gave new voice to an ancient dream:

> To become a true Russian, to become a Russian fully, means only to become the brother of all men, to become, if you will, a universal man, and in the course of time I believe that we, not we of course but our children to come, will all without exception understand that to be a true Russian does indeed mean to

aspire to reconcile finally the contradictions of Europe, to find a way out for the yearning for Europe in our Russian soul, pan-human and all-uniting, to include within our soul by brotherly love all our brethren and at last, it may be, to pronounce the final word of the great general harmony of the final brotherly communion of all nations in accordance with the law of the gospel of Christ. I know, I know too well, that my words may appear ecstatic, exaggerated, and fantastic. Let them be so. I do not repent having uttered them.

Under the Tsars, Russia's universal mission and global aspirations were represented by the orthodox Church and later by Pan-Slavism, as they are now represented under the Soviets by "international Communism." Under the Tsars, Russia's secular and temporal power was represented by the Romanov Autocracy, as it is now represented by the Soviet State.

These two aspects of Russia's role in the world are interestingly and somewhat amusingly symbolized by two historical curiosities which stand near to one another inside the Kremlin walls in Moscow. One is the largest bell in the world, the Tsar Bell, cast in 1735, symbolizing religion and ideology and Holy Russia's universal mission. The other is the largest brass cannon in the world, the Tsar Cannon, cast in 1586, symbolizing Russia's secular power and military might. The amusing thing is that the Tsar Bell was never rung after the first two years, because it was so heavy it fell out of the belltower and cracked, and has been sitting cracked on the ground ever since. The Tsar cannon was never fired. It would have fallen to pieces had any effort been made to fire it, as the forgers well knew. It was made as an artifact without function to impress and frighten foreign ambassadors and visitors to Moscow.

The cult of Marxism borrowed from the West is the latest variant of the age-old Russian mission of universalism, based on Muscovite power but offering to all men and women everywhere an all-embracing gospel of deliverance through subjection to the one true faith. Russian foreign policy in its Soviet form is the latest variant of the age-old Russian mission, verbalized in terms of the prevailing gospel, of protecting and promoting the interests of Muscovy in its contacts of war and peace with the other members of the modern State System.

Now I venture to offer a hypothesis regarding Russian attitudes and policies toward the West.

The hypothesis is that these attitudes and policies cannot be adequately understood by concentrating our attention on Russian secular power, Russia's national interests and ambitions, and what we like to call "Soviet imperialism," or by concentrating our attention exclusively on Russia's universal mission, Russia's messianic complex, or what we call "international Communism." Both of these, "Soviet imperialism" and "international Communism," are new forms of very old purposes in the Russian community. In order to understand them both, to comprehend their past and to forecast their future, we must take full account not only of the past forty-five years but also Russia's age-old experience, much of it tragic, through many centuries. Then we must ask ourselves now what has changed and what is the same in the underlying sources or causes of Russian attitudes and policies toward the West.

Within my limited time, talent, and knowledge I cannot hope to state these sources or causes of attitudes and policies with full adequacy and precision. But I can make an effort in the form of a series of broad propositions or generalizations, even though we cannot document each of these fully. As you give critical attention to these efforts, please bear in mind always the old French proverb that all generalizations are false, including the generalization that all generalizations are false.

The *first* of these generalizations or propositions is this: In comparison with America and with the Western European Great Powers, that Power known successively as the Grand Duchy of Muscovy, the Russian Empire, and the Soviet Union has always been, until quite recently, economically backward and therefore militarily weak to the degree to which military might is a function of economic progress and abundant productivity. This backwardness and weakness of the Russian community has been attributed by some to an inhospitable climate, by others to the great plains and the grey masses, and by still others to the "Russian soul" or to defects of Russian character. I prefer to believe from the record that this backwardness and weakness are chiefly attributable to the impact and consequences for the Russian community of the Mongol conquest and the Mongol yoke which, for two and one-half centuries, from 1240 to 1480— longer than the whole period of American independence thus far—tended to isolate Russia from the cultural stimulation of Western medieval civilization and from the beginnings of the Renaissance and the Reformation.

Second proposition: While America, protected by the Atlantic Ocean from superior European land Powers, expanded westward over an empty continent in relative security against external attack, the Russian community, expanding eastward over an empty continent, was at all times exposed to, and relatively defenseless against, external attack by the major land Powers of Europe. Once freed from the Mongol yoke, Russia was obliged repeatedly to fight for national survival against formidable foes to the north, to the west, to the south. Disunity and weakness in the heart of Muscovy have usually led to invasion or intervention from abroad—by Swedes, Germans, Lithuanians, and Poles in the Mongol period, since the Mongols were little interested in the western frontiers; by Turkey, Poland, and Sweden in the late sixteenth, seventeenth, and early eighteenth centuries; by France in the early nineteenth century; by France and Britain in the mid-nineteenth century; by Japan in the early twentieth century; by Germany in World War I; by Poland, France, Britain, Japan, and America after World War I; by Germany, Italy, and their allies in World War II.

These invasions and interventions have been more frequent, more destructive, more costly, more tragic, than those which have afflicted any other major national community in modern times. In each case, I have no doubt, the invaders or interventionists asserted and believed that their conduct was wholly justified by Russian provocation or by Russian sin or by Russian weakness. In each case patriotic Russians believed that their bitter misfortunes were due to national disunity and backwardness in the face of stronger and hostile Powers.

Third proposition: The age-old responses of the rulers of Russia, and indeed of the people of Russia, to the double challenge of internal weakness and external aggression, centuries before Communism was ever heard of, have been, in the first place, political autocracy; in the second place, ideological orthodoxy and intolerance; in the third place, territorial expansionism on an immense scale; in the fourth place, messianic universalism; and in the fifth place, Westernization or industrialization sponsored by the State in a frantic and almost desperate series of efforts to catch up with and, if possible, surpass the nation-states of the West in economic development.

By and large, the rulers of Russia who sought to push economic development were not interested in economic development for purposes of human welfare or the raising of living standards. They were interested in economic development as a means of enhancing military power, and this goal was usually envisaged, and rightly envisaged, as the price of national survival. This was the program of Ivan the Great in the fifteenth century. This was the program of Ivan the Terrible in the sixteenth century. This was the program of Peter the Great in the late seventeenth and early eighteenth centuries. This was, in part at least, the program of Catherine the Great in the later eighteenth century. This was the program of the more enlightened of the nineteenth-century Russian Tsars. This was the program of Stalin in the twentieth century. And this is the program of Khrushchev as Stalin's successor.

The pattern of response which I am citing is very old indeed. It is centuries old. In terms of this particular portion of our hypothesis, the most illuminating single statement on Russian attitudes and policies toward the West since the October Revolution was undoubtedly the statement made by Stalin to the first All-Union Conference of Managers of Socialist Industry on February 4, 1931, in the middle of the first Five-Year Plan, almost ten years after the final end of the Allied and American military intervention in World War I and almost exactly ten years before the Nazi invasion of World War II. Said Stalin in 1931:

> Those who fall behind get beaten, but we do not want to be beaten. We refuse to be beaten. Old Russia was beaten by the Mongol Khans; she was beaten by the Turkish Beys; she was beaten by the Swedish feudal lords; she was beaten by the Polish and Lithuanian gentry; she was beaten by the British and French capitalists; she was beaten by the Japanese barons; all beat her—for her backwardness, for military backwardness, for cultural backwardness, for political backwardness, for industrial backwardness, for agricultural backwardness. She was beaten because it was profitable, and it could be done with impunity. Do you remember the words of the pre-revolutionary poet: "You are poor and abundant, mighty and impotent, Mother Russia"? These words of the old poet were well learned by those gentlemen. They beat her. Such is the law of the exploiters—to beat the backward and the weak. That is why we must no longer lag behind. You must put an end to backwardness in the shortest possible· time and develop genuine Bolshevik tempo in building up the socialist system of economy.

> There is no other way. Either we do it or they
> crush us.

I do not quote the late Josef Vissarionovich Dju-gashvili, better known to us as Stalin, for the purpose of expressing approval of his words. I quote him by way of indicating that here again the Russian response to Western challenge, the Russian response to internal backwardness and weakness, is a very old one.

A *fourth proposition* may be added: In the great tests of power Russia's rulers, when they have acted wisely, have not taken the initiative in precipitating a trial by arms but have left the initiative to the enemy, even when such passivity was certain to put the nation in a strategically dangerous position. This attitude is doubtless attributable again in part to backwardness and weakness and to repeated demonstrations over the centuries that the Russian masses fight heroically and effectively in defense of the Motherland against alien aggression and seldom fight heroically and effectively in hostilities initiated by Russian action. Thus Russian policy-makers, after the obvious breakdown of the truce of Tilsit with Napoleon, left it to the Emperor of France to unleash war in 1812. Although Russian policy-makers, by ordering general mobilization and ignoring the German ultimatum, did in a sense precipitate war in 1914, they nevertheless left it to Germany to declare war on Russia on August 1, 1914. The Marxist leaders in 1917 and 1918 sought peace with the Allied and Associated Powers and left to them the inauguration of hostilities. They did likewise in dealing with Poland in the spring of 1920. And, most notably, Russia's policy-makers, although some of them had known for many months in the spring of 1941 that the Axis assault was impending, and although enormous military advantages could have been gained by attacking while much of the Nazi Wehrmacht was occupied in Yugoslavia and Greece, nevertheless again left it to Hitler and Mussolini to open the conflict.

This generalization suggests a possibly valid corollary having to do with so-called "preventive" wars which are now more politely called "pre-emptive" wars. But I prefer the old adjective. The corollary suggested by the record is simply this: When Russian policy-makers initiate preventive wars, Russia is defeated; when others initiate preventive wars against Russia, they are sometimes successful when they pursue limited political or territorial aims, as for example, in 1854 and in 1904; but they are invariably defeated when they pursue total and unlimited purposes aiming at the conquest or destruction of the Russian State, as in 1812 and 1919 and 1941.

The *fifth proposition*—which you may find less credible than the others—is that the major territorial aggrandizements of Russia in Europe (I speak now not of Asia) have been more often a result of unsuccessful military aggression against Russia by Western Powers than a result of successful military aggression by Russia against Western Powers. Thus Swedish, Lithuanian, Polish, and Turkish seizures of formerly Russian territories during the Mongol subjugation of six hundred years ago, and the Polish occupation of Moscow during the "Time of Troubles" three hundred years ago, both led ultimately to Russian recovery of all the lost provinces and to Russian seizure of formerly Swedish, Lithuanian, Polish, and Turkish territories. Thus Napoleon's invasion of Russia in 1812 culminated not only in the downfall of the Napoleonic Empire but also in appreciable enlargement of Russian territory in Europe. The Allied invasion of Russia in 1918 and 1919 and the Polish invasion of 1920 likewise eventuated in the establishment of Russian sovereignty over more extensive territories than would have passed under Russian sovereignty had these invasions not been launched.

The contemporary post-World War II increments of Soviet territory and influence, although popularly and officially attributed in America to Soviet or Communist "aggression" or "imperialism," are once more in part an aftermath of Western aggression against Russia.

For a period of eighteen years, from 1921 to 1939, when Western military aggression against Russia was not indulged in and not overtly threatened, there was no Russian territorial aggrandizement at all. The Soviet acquisitions of 1939–1940, achieved by Russian intervention in Poland, by threatened Russian aggression against Estonia, Latvia, and Lithuania, and also against Rumania, and by overt Russian military aggression against Finland, were all motivated by an almost desperate necessity for strengthening Russia's defenses against an anticipated attack, sooner or later, from the Nazi Reich and its Fascist allies. The further territorial acquisitions of 1944 and 1945 and the vast extension of Soviet influence over adjacent territories would very obviously never have taken place by Russian initiative except for the murderous assault of Fascist Europe on Russia and the subsequent defeat and collapse of Fascist Europe at the hands of the United Nations coalition, after a frightful conflict in which Russia suffered at least ten times the human and material losses of all the other members of the United Nations combined.

It is nevertheless true that the expansion of Russian power over eight and one-half million square miles, or one-sixth of the land surface of the planet, and further expansions beyond this huge area have quite understandably and justifiably aroused acute alarm among Western peoples and governments, fearful of their security and persuaded that the rulers of Russia were bent on conquering all the world. This again is a theme or *motif* which is much older than the Russian Revolution and dates back many centuries. Someone once calculated that the Russian Empire under the Tsars expanded its territory at an average rate of sixty square miles a day for three hundred years. That adds up to a very appreciable amount of territory. More recently, to cite one more or less random example of Western responses to Russian territorial aggrandizement, Paul G. Hoffman, who was then head of International Cooperation Administration, said in a press conference in New York on January 6, 1949, over a dozen years ago now:

> Hitler was a baby compared with this gang. He didn't know what it was all about. When you see the countries they have taken over and when you see what they have done in

China, you realize what a menace this power drive is. Let's not talk about it as the spread of Communism; let's talk about it for what it is—an attempt by the gang in the Politburo to take over the world.

Another earlier authority wrote more explicitly, and rather more eloquently, as follows:

Pan-Slavism is a movement which endeavors to undo what a thousand-year-old history has created. It cannot achieve its aim without sweeping Turkey, Hungary, and half of Germany off the map of Europe. Should this result ever be accomplished, it could be made to last by no other means than the subjugation of Europe. Pan-Slavism has now transformed itself from an article of faith into a political program. By now it is no longer only Russia but the whole Pan-Slavistic plot which threatens to found its realm on the ruins of Europe. This leaves Europe only one alternative—subjugation through slavery or lasting destruction of the center of its offensive strength.

The words I have just quoted were written in the year 1855 by a journalist and scholar whose name was Karl Marx. Now, of course, Karl Marx was wrong a century ago in asserting that the conquest of Europe by Tsarist Russia could be prevented only by the destruction of Russia, just as Paul Hoffman was wrong in assuming that the rulers of Soviet Russia had either the intention or the capacity to take over the world.

Yet Russian aggrandizement and messianism long before the October Revolution repeatedly gave rise to great fear abroad, and that fear in recent years, when Russia has vast new power at its disposal, is more acute than ever before, particularly in America, since human beings in general, and perhaps Russians in particular, are always tempted to abuse vast new power. I would not argue for a moment that this fear is completely irrational or altogether unwarranted or unnecessary. We would be well advised indeed to look to our security, providing we do so sanely and wisely.

But I should want to argue that the vast new power which Russia now possesses, forty-five years after the October Revolution, is in itself a product of a radical transformation of the Russian community and a drastic alteration in the age-old pattern of relationships between Russia and the West. And I would further argue that out of these immense changes of circumstances we may reasonably expect major changes in the old responses of the Russian community to the West. These changes, I venture to believe, will be constructive, not destructive, and conducive to hope rather than despair. Many of them are already under way, if only we will take off our old blinders and look at them. In its fifth decade after the October Revolution, the Russia of the Seven-Year Plan is no longer a weak and backward nation, threatened with attack by other Powers and driven toward autocracy, intolerance, aggrandizement, and messianism by its very weakness, backwardness, and formlessness. The Russia of today is a powerful, prosperous, and advanced nation. No other Power, not even America, is going to attack Russia, not unless Americans become so frightened that they lose their minds, which I do not anticipate.

Are Russian political autocracy and despotism a product of weakness, poverty, and ignorance? I believe so. The Russia of today is strong, flourishing, and literate, highly industrialized, highly urbanized, and extraordinarily well-educated. Therefore, autocracy and despotism are obsolete; Stalinism is obsolete. Therefore, Stalin's successors must strive, as they have been striving, to liberalize the Communist Party and, in at least some measure, democratize Soviet government and put an end to Stalin's police-state terrorism. They have no choice; they have been moving ahead with this task. There can be no return to Stalinism in Russia. All the movement of change is quite in the other direction.

Are ideological orthodoxy and intolerance also products of weakness, poverty, and ignorance? I believe so, in part at any rate. By the same token, an educated, prosperous, and powerful Russian community, which is more and more a middleclass or bourgeois community, despite the absence of private property, must inevitably relax political intolerance and party-line orthodoxy and move toward greater freedom of speech, press, and assembly and greater public participation in public policy-making. And this is happening. It has been happening now for several years.

Are Russian expansionism and territorial aggrandizement products of fear of attack from abroad and of the repeated fact of attack from abroad? Again, I believe so. If so, then we may expect a diminution of expansionism and aggrandizement *pari passu* with a diminution of fear of foreign attack. Indeed, even in the bad old days of the evil Stalin, our own Western fears of Russian military aggression and attempts at world conquest were, we may say with the wisdom of hindsight, rather exaggerated. On this I limit myself to quoting only two distinguished American authorities. One of these well-known authorities, speaking in 1949 before the Third National Conference on Churches and World Order, put the matter in these words. Perhaps he later ignored or forgot the validity of these words, but these were his words in March of 1949: "So far as it is humanly possible to judge, the Soviet Government under conditions now prevailing does not contemplate the use of war as an instrument of its national policy. I do not know any responsible high official, military or civilian, in this government or any government who believes that the Soviet Government now plans conquest by open military aggression." The speaker of those words was the late John Foster Dulles.

The other American authority I would cite is George Frost Kennan, former ambassador in Moscow, now ambassador to Belgrade. Kennan, writing in the August, 1956, issue of *Harper's* on what he called "Overdue Changes in Our Foreign Policy," made the comment (and I think most of you are aware of the fact that, if there are a half-dozen people in the United States who really know something about Russia, George Kennan is one of them) that there had prevailed in this country "a rather common impression that Stalin was a man of war aiming to launch a military onslaught against the non-Communist world and deterred only by our atomic armaments."

> This is a great oversimplification. Stalin was not what you would call a nice man, and his intentions toward ourselves were strictly dishonorable. But those intentions, I am convinced, did not include the determination to unleash a third World War in the grand manner. The image of a Stalinist Russia poised and yearning to attack the West, and deterred only by our possession of atomic weapons, was largely a creation of the Western imagination, against which some of us who were familiar with Russian matters tried in vain over the course of the years to make our voices heard.

At all events, it is the conclusion of the argument here being advanced that the transformation of the Russian community during the past thirty years from a poor, ignorant, weak, and backward society into a relatively wealthy, literate, strong, and advanced society, highly educated, highly industrialized, and highly urbanized, will have, and is in fact having, two consequences which are hopeful for the future. One is the progressive liberalization and democratization of the Soviet polity and of Soviet society. The other is the emergence of a pattern, or at least of the possibility of a pattern, of stable and peaceful relations between Russia and the West. Whether in fact this possibility will be realized and this hope will be fulfilled will depend obviously upon the wisdom of Western statesmanship and of Russian statesmanship during the weeks and months and years which lie before us.

Lecture Two

The Social Order

IN ACCORDANCE WITH A PECULIAR PERSONAL CUS-tom which I like sometimes to honor more in the observance than in the breach, I take my text for this second lecture from my favorite book on world politics, as follows:

"Very true," said the Duchess. "Flamingos and mustard both bite. And the moral of that is: birds of a feather flock together."

"Only mustard isn't a bird," Alice remarked.

"Right as usual," said the Duchess. "What a clear way you have of putting things."

"It's a mineral, I think," said Alice.

"Of course it is," said the Duchess, who seemed ready to agree to everything that Alice said. "There's a large mustard mine near here and the moral of that is: the more there is of mine, the less there is of yours."

"Oh, I know," exclaimed Alice, who had not attended to this last remark, "it's a vegetable. It doesn't look like one, but it is."

"I quite agree with you," said the Duchess, "and the moral of that is: be what you would seem to be or, if you would like it put more simply, never imagine yourself not to be otherwise than what it might appear to others that you were or might have been was not otherwise than what you had been would have appeared to them to be otherwise."

I am sure you would all agree that mustard can be most unpleasant and even dangerous if incorrectly labeled or wrongly identified, although relatively harmless when correctly labeled and rightly identified. Communism is much more dangerous and much less tangible than mustard and is somewhat more difficult, for some people at least, to identify rightly or to label correctly. So great is the difficulty that many of us quite understandably are content with catchwords. We find it easy, for example, to say and believe that Communism is totalitarianism; that Fascism, which we also failed to understand until almost too late, is also totalitarianism; that therefore Communism is Red Fascism or, more simply, that Communism is Fascism. Some among us say that Communism is un-American. Others among us say that un-Americanism is Communism. None of these formulations is very helpful or very clarifying. It is true, according to Aristotle and Euclid, that things equal to the same thing are equal to each other. This proposition is of impeccable validity in mathematics. But I fear it is of most questionable validity in politics and in other human affairs.

I would invite you to reconsider the meaning of Communism on the assumption, which I hope and believe is valid, that one must understand one's enemy if one is to oppose one's enemy successfully. There may be truth in the old French proverb "who understands all forgives all," and there may even be truth in the much older Christian and Jewish advice to "love one's enemies." But these injunctions, as we all know, may be highly inexpedient and dangerous in international politics where it is very hazardous to forgive one's enemies or to love one's enemies. But there is one thing more hazardous than either of these, and that is to be ignorant of one's enemies.

We are agreed, surely, that Communism is the enemy. We need to understand the enemy in order to know how the enemy may best be opposed. We need further to understand the Communist ideology as a means of understanding the political, economic, and social order which has been brought into being by the Communist rulers of the Soviet Union. Communism, like most other phenomena of human conduct labeled by words ending in "-ism," is a system of beliefs about the universe and the world and a system of values and purposes in human affairs existing inside the minds and hearts of various and sundry men and women. These beliefs and values cannot be comprehended by labeling them good, true, or beautiful, or by labeling them evil, false, or ugly. Communism can best be understood, I would suggest, as a cult and must be faced and understood and, if possible, defeated or restricted or contained as a cult.

I would not use the word "religion" here, because in most of its usages, the word religion implies belief in a personal God or gods and in a life after death. Devotees of the cult of Communism deny the Deity and deny immortality. Nevertheless, for its disciples Communism is yet a kind of religion, as all of us know who as infidel tourists have visited the Kremlin or the tomb on Red Square. Communism is, in that sense, a kind of religion or at least a kind of sacred cult. Its disciples emotionally identify its beliefs and values with their own conception, distorted as it may be, of the good, the true, and the beautiful; and they regard its doctrines as the clue to the mysteries of the Cosmos, of the World, and of Man. This is why the world's greatest living philosopher, Bertrand Russell, has called Communism "the fourth of the Judaic higher religion" and why the world's greatest living historian, Arnold J. Toynbee, has called Communism "the great Jewish-Christian heresy of our time."

Indeed the resemblance of Communism as an ideology to other major cults in past human experience is even more striking than has here been suggested. All of the higher religions of mankind, and many of mankind's more influential social and political cults, furnish to their converts an emotionally satisfying set of symbols which fortify belief, motivate conduct, and promote peace of mind and peace of soul. These symbols usually include the figure of a bearded prophet; a galaxy of heroes, saints, and martyrs; and a sacred book, ponderous, obscure, ambiguous, read by few, understood by fewer, but revered by all as a revelation. The symbols include a doctrine of the origin of things, the meaning of things, and the end of things. The symbols usually include a millennial apocalyptic vision of sin, repentance, judgment day, and salvation.

The Communist or Marxist ideology has all of these symbols in abundance. The bearded prophet is Karl Marx. His ideologically begotten son is Lenin. The heroes, saints, and martyrs are those who fought and died for the liberation of the proletariat from capitalism. The sacred book is *Das Kapital,* supplemented by other writings. The censors of Tsarist Russia permitted the first translation of *Das Kapital* from German into Russian in 1872 on the ground that the book was harmless because totally unreadable. They were quite correct, albeit politically mistaken. The doctrine of beginnings and ends is "dialectical materialism" or, as applied to human affairs, "historical materialism." The millennial and apocalyptic vision is, of course, the collapse of capitalism and a transition to socialism and ultimately to pure economic communism by way of the proletarian revolution, the dictatorship of the proletariat, the building of social-ism, the withering away of the State, and the ulti-mate attainment of something like heaven on earth through the co-operative commonwealth in which all coercion or exploitation of men by men will vanish and the willing labor of each will contribute to the common welfare of all.

Notice that this cult, unlike most versions of Christianity, is not a cult of individual salvation in a life beyond the grave but is a cult of social salvation in the life before the grave. Men and women will not delight in heaven or suffer in hell, but they will satisfy all their needs here and now. Notice also that the cult of Communism shares some moral values and social ideals with Christianity, Judaism, Islam, and Western liberalism or democracy—namely, the goal of human equality and brotherhood in One World. Other values and ideals, and above all practices, of Communism are wholly antithetical to the Jewish-Christian liberal tradition—political dictatorship, ideological orthodoxy and intolerance, negation of individual freedom and personal dignity, and the al-ways stultifying doctrine that the end justifies the means.

Now there is no possibility, and happily no necessity, to expound here the ideological doctrines of Communism as originally set forth in the writings of Karl Marx and Friedrich Engels and subsequently elaborated in the writings of Lenin, Stalin, Khrushchev, and hundreds of non-Russian Marxists. Whole libraries of books have been written and published and read on Marxism as a philosophy of the Cosmos, as a theory of history, as a system of sociology, as a doctrine of economics, as a science of politics, as a vision of the millennium, and as a formula for human salvation. Neither is there any possibility nor necessity for me to offer a refutation of Marxism. Here again whole libraries of books have been written and published and read for the purpose of demonstrating that Marxism is philosophically wrong, that it is sociologically wrong, that it is economically wrong, that it is politically wrong, and that it is spiritually wrong. And so indeed it is, in many respects, and I have myself contributed a good deal to that literature—which I presume is why *Pravda* in its issue of October 23, 1953, said that I was a "tool of Wall Street" and an American "warmonger" and "imperialist."

All of this, from one point of view, would be a waste of time and energy, somewhat comparable to efforts at refuting Judaism, Christianity, Islam, Buddhism, Hinduism, or Confucianism. Where there is a will to believe and a need for faith, logical refutations of any creed or cult which appeals to the aspirations of many people have no effect whatever on the converts of the cult and not very much on the potential converts to the cult. Human beings do not, it seems to me, live and act by reason alone, as Marxists assume and as most democrats and liberals assume. Human beings live in terms of their hopes and their fears, their loyalties, their aspirations, their ambitions, their purposes, and their dedication and devotion to what they believe and what they want to believe and to what they love or what they want to love. Refuting Marxism is comparable to what Mark Twain once said about giving up smoking. He said that "giving up smoking is the easiest thing in the world. I've done it hundreds of times." So it is with refutations of Marxism. The task has been done not hundreds but thousands of times and it has no effect whatever, precisely because Marxism has long since become a creed and a cult, the disciples of which have no interest in logical demonstrations that their beliefs are false.

Therefore, I shall not pursue this particular line of thought but instead pursue a rather different theme which I believe to be more interesting and

significant in our efforts to understand the Soviet
Union. Let me state the theme in the form of a very
broad and complicated question. Given the beliefs
and hopes and fears and expectations and aspirations
of the Russian Marxists or Communists who made
themselves rulers of Russia in the October Revolution of 1917, what have they made of the Russia they
have ruled for the past forty-five years? How and
why and what is the relationship between the present structure and prospective structure of Soviet society and the original beliefs and aspirations of the
Russian Marxists? What may we reasonably expect
to emerge in the Russia of the years which lie ahead?
This is a very large question, indeed, which admits
of no final or definitive answer. Yet we may alleviate
our ignorance slightly by devoting some time and
thought to trying to find partial answers to this very
broad question.

Russian Marxists, like all Marxists from the very
beginning of their movement and especially during
the early years of the twentieth century, were con-
fronted with a paradox or dilemma posed by the
very precepts of the Marxist ideology. This paradox stemmed from the Marxist premise—which we
can readily see was a false premise—that the collapse of capitalism, the proletarian revolution, and

the ultimate transition by way of the so-called "dicta-torship of the proletariat" toward a socialist economy and ultimately a communist economy were all things which could come to pass only in mature, advanced, highly industrialized, highly urbanized, and there-fore decadent capitalist societies. This was for long a Marxist article of faith. But the Russia of 1917 was not at all a mature, advanced, highly industrialized, highly urbanized, and decadent society. On the con-trary, the Russia of 1917 was still a primitive semi-feudal, illiterate, rural, or agrarian society in which industrial capitalism had made a very modest begin-ning. How then were the Russian Marxists to define their own mission? And how were they to justify their seizure of power and for what purposes were they to use the power that they had seized?

These questions led to much agonizing and bit-ter disputation among Russian Marxists for ten years and more before the October Revolution of 1917 and for ten years and more after the October Revolution of 1917. The details of these controversies are be-yond our present purview. Suffice it to say that the Marxist rulers of Russia resolved their dilemma in three ways, each of which has been enormously por-tentous for Russia and for all the world in the middle decades of the twentieth century. One of these ways, and a way which all of us in the West have deemed most dangerous and menacing, was embodied in the Communist formula and hope of "World Revolution," or as Trotsky preferred to call it, "permanent revolution." Lenin and his Marxist colleagues long before 1917 persuaded themselves by virtue of their Marxist dogma that socialist revolution in backward Russia could have no chance of success or survival unless the European proletariats of the advanced capitalist countries, Germany, France, and England, should rise in revolution against the bourgeoisie, establish "dictatorships of the proletariat" in their own countries, and somehow come to the aid of the Marxist rulers of backward Russia. This hope, of course, proved vain since Marx and Lenin were wrong in their prognosis of the ultimate development of Western capitalism.

The second way in which the Russian Marxists resolved their dilemma was to bring into being in 1918 and 1919 the first totalitarian police-state of our time, later copied for quite other purposes by Mussolini, Hitler, Franco, and the Japanese warlords. This solution of the problem of the Russian Marxists, which all of us in the West deemed deplorable, abhorrent, and monstrous, was not implicit in the ideology of Marxism despite Marx's talk of the "dictatorship of the proletariat" and his quaint notion that the revolutionary Paris Commune of 1871 was somehow an embodiment of his ideal as to the form of government that should prevail in the revolutionary time to come. In fact, if we study the record, we will discover that the Soviet totalitarian police-state was no part of the program or purpose of the Russian Marxists who seized power in the October Revolution of 1917, and we will further discover that the Soviet regime in 1917–1918, however you may choose to describe it, could not possibly be described as a totalitarian police-state. What it might have become had it been left alone, we shall never know. It was not left alone.

In the summer of 1918 other Powers—the United States, Britain, France, Italy, Japan, and lesser States —sent invading armies into Russia to support the White Armies fighting the Red Armies and to overthrow the Soviet regime. These efforts failed, due in part to patriotic Russian support of the Red regime against the White Armies and the Allied and American interventionists. The failure was also due to the invention by the Russian Marxists of the first totalitarian police-state of our age as a means of defense against domestic and foreign foes in a civil war which was also an international war.

The third way in which the Russian Marxists resolved their dilemma was to apply the methods of the totalitarian police-state to a grandiose program for the socialist industrialization of Russia inaugurated in 1928 with the first Five-Year Plan. This program was long deferred and was the subject of bitter debates among the Russian Marxists. Amid chaos and almost total economic collapse, Lenin in 1921 had sponsored and put through the so-called New Economic Policy, which he described as a "strategic retreat toward capitalism." Lenin died on January 21, 1924. His wrangling successors discussed and quarreled and ultimately killed one another in controversy over "where do we go from here." The Autocracy of Stalin the Terrible finally emerged.

Bear in mind that after the fearful tragedies of death and ruin which overwhelmed Russia in World War I—revolution, civil war, more foreign war, famine, and almost fatal economic paralysis—Russian agriculture and industry did not recover to their 1913 level of output until 1927, during the era of the New Economic Policy. Only then did the Communist

Party under Stalin's increasingly despotic leadership embark upon massive industrialization and the collectivization of agriculture. Both purposes were ruthlessly pushed forward under the first Five-Year Plan, with tragic and horrible results in terms of the material and human costs of the program. What ensued, however, was of enormous importance for all Russia and for all the world.

Let me try to put what ensued in rather simple human terms by way of a fairly long, but I hope not tedious, quotation from one of the books of John Scott, who spent five years in Siberia under the second Five-Year Plan and in recent years has been the brilliant editorial assistant and research aide of James Linen, publisher of *Time* magazine. Scott was not corrupted by his five-year stay in Siberia. In his book *Behind the Urals* he described in concrete human terms what was transpiring on an immense scale in the desperate Russia of the 1930's:

> I arrived in Magnitogorsk on the eastern slopes of the Ural mountains in the fall of 1932 and went to work on blast furnace construction. A week or so later another young man came to work in the same gang. His name was Shaimat. Shaimat was a Tartar. He

left his village because he had heard that in Magnitogorsk his bread ration would be larger than it was at home. When he arrived, he had never seen an electric light, a stair case, or a locomotive. He had seen a hammer but he had never used one. The only hammering he had ever done was to drive a tent stake into the ground with a rock. He did not wash and had many lice. Shaimat was sent to our gang by the plant personnel office in response to an urgent request by our foreman for an electrician. Shaimat had no such qualifications, of course, but he was a man.

Kolya the foreman cursed colorfully when he found that Shaimat spoke no Russian, only his native Tartar, and was completely illiterate. But he put him to work in a booth where a half-dozen German AC motor generators were grinding out direct current for welding. When the bulb in the ceiling went out, as it often did because of breakdowns in the powerhouse or on the line, Shaimat was to turn off the motors, then switch them on again in two stages when the juice came back. During his first day, Shaimat burned out two motors. He followed through with three more several days later.

For a month or more he sat humming to himself some doleful Tartar tune or gaping up at the blast furnaces and coke ovens without any comprehension at all of what it was all about. He had come to Magnitogorsk for that thousand gram bread card. He was getting it and seemed content.

But then Shaimat began doing two things. First he began to learn the Russian language by a sort of osmosis and started to converse with the others in the gang and in the barracks at night. Second, he was organized into a course for adult illiterates. Nearly every barracks had such a course and he began to learn to read. As he struggled through his first simple newspapers and as he talked with those around him, his horizon suddenly broadened.

He learned that Magnitogorsk was one of the major construction jobs of the Five-Year Plan, that its equipment had been bought in America and Germany in exchange for some hundred million dollars worth of Soviet butter and cloth and furs and wheat which was why he, Shaimat, was frequently hungry and never well clothed. He learned that already the plant was producing half as much pig iron as all of Russia in 1913. He was told and believed that the plant belonged to him and that ultimately he would get his steel in nails and rails and perhaps a bicycle.

As he learned these things, Shaimat grew to like his work. He learned to curse the men in the powerhouse when the juice went off and the gang stood idle. He learned that it was cultured to smear his spittle with his feet when he spit on the floor. He learned to attend the trade union meetings and use his activity to get an extra meal card for the dining room. He also learned something of the nature of an electric motor. As months became years, Shaimat changed rapidly. By 1937 he was going to night school, learning about amperes and ergs. He could rewind his motors when they burned out. He read books and magazines. He washed himself all over in the banya once a week. He had no lice and his clothes were neatly patched and fairly clean. He could solve quadratic equations and he knew that Joseph Stalin, the great white father in Moscow, was responsible for these many blessings.

Of course Shaimat was crude, stubborn, and one-sided, but his way of life had changed more in his five years in Magnitogorsk than that of his Tartar ancestors since the days of Tamerlane. He had been picked up by the scruff of the neck from a medieval village and dropped into a relatively modern industrial town with all the complicated technical and social problems one finds in such cities all over the world, and Shaimat had survived. Many of his friends and fellow workmen did not survive. They died of typhus, froze in the sub-zero temperatures in winter. They fell from

scaffolds; they dropped things on one another's heads. They ran afoul of the sleepless
NKVD and got themselves shot. There were
many hazards to which millions succumbed.
But tens of millions like Shaimat survived and
worked hard, excited with their new opportunities, hopeful of a better life in years to
come.

In short, the Stalinist program for the industrialization of Russia was ultimately successful. By trial
and error, accompanied by appalling waste, frightful
mistakes, and hideous injustices and crimes, the
Communist Party of the Soviet Union finally suc-
ceeded in inventing a totally socialized and totally
planned national economy, quite different from the
business systems of Western countries, which in the
end was to become enormously productive. Its productivity stemmed from a new method of capital accumulation based principally upon the turnover tax,
whereby Soviet consumers pay roughly double the
price for the goods they buy in relation to the cost of
producing and distributing the goods. Stemming
also from a new method of capital investment organized through the Gosplan or State Planning Commission, these new inventions in the organization of
business activity have enabled the Soviet economy
to expand its output at an average rate of about 8 per

cent per year (in industrial output) compared to an average rate of growth in the United States and Western Europe to 2 to 4 per cent a year, except in periods of very exceptional prosperity.

The Soviet formula for rapid industrialization and rapid economic growth has an enormous appeal to the poverty-stricken peoples of Asia, Africa, and Latin America, all striving for industrialization and Western living standards. The Soviet formula for rapid industrialization and rapid economic growth also explains how Russia was able in World War II to win final victory over Nazi Europe and, despite incredible devastation and unbelievable human losses, to restore the productivity of Russian industry and agriculture by 1950 to the levels of 1940 and then to move forward to greater achievements.

But it is important to note here that the very success of the Stalinist economic program doomed to obsolescence the Stalinist scheme of political power, operating by the methods of the totalitarian police-state. The successful industrialization of Russia meant the urbanization of Russia and the mass education of Russia. Stalin could rule as tyrant over a poor, illiterate, and rural Russia. No new Stalin can rule as tyrant over a relatively rich, literate, and urban Russia.

Stalin's successors as rulers of Russia—Malenkov, Bulganin, and Khrushchev, who has, of course, relegated his predecessors to the doghouse—have all been grappling with the problem of how to adapt the political methods of a totalitarian police-state to the needs and requirements of a relatively prosperous, urbanized, and well-educated Russia where the methods of the totalitarian police-state are no longer applicable or operationally workable. Their solution of the problem thus far has not involved any modification of the oligarchy of the Communist Party, which continues to enjoy a so-called "monopoly of legality," nor any real democratization of the formal structure and functioning of Soviet government.

Their solution thus far has involved the following changes in Stalinist system of power, some of which are quite drastic: (1) the downgrading of the political police, symbolized by the arrest and execution of Beria in 1953 and the end of the police-state terrorism; (2) the liberalization and democratization of the Communist Party itself in the sense that the Presidium or, as it was once called, "Politburo" of the Party and the Central Committee of the Party, along in lesser measure with the Congresses of the Party, now debate and vote on issues of public policy as they never did in Stalin's last years, and thus reach decisions which are "collective" and far more "democratic" than they ever were in the era of the Stalinist tyranny; and (3) the enactment of new civil and criminal codes of law and various judicial reforms which give to the Soviet citizen at the present time much more assurance of his legal rights and of objective justice in the Western sense than he has ever known before. And these are all beginnings, not endings, of a process.

Meanwhile, the totally socialized and totally planned economy of the Soviet Union has continued to flourish, to the regret of many of us. Statistics are boring to most Americans and fascinating to most Russians, but I will run the risk of citing a few statistics. Under the fifth Five-Year Plan of 1950–1955 production in heavy industry exceeded somewhat the goals set by the Plan. By 1955 Soviet production of steel came to 45 million metric tons; of pig iron to 33 million metric tons; of coal to 390 million tons; of oil to 70 million tons. The sixth Five-Year Plan contemplated targets of 50 million tons of pig iron and 60 million tons of steel in 1960. This Plan was abandoned in 1958 in favor of the current Seven-Year Plan of 1959–1965, not so much, it seems to me, because of any real failure to achieve the output targets, but rather because of emergent possibilities of achieving a better balanced program of industrial and agricultural growth. The original Seven-Year Plan, like the sixth Five-Year Plan, aimed at 50 million tons of pig iron and 60 million tons of steel in 1960. In fact, Soviet industrial output in 1960 seems to have increased by 10 per cent as against a planned increase of 8 per cent, with steel production in 1960 at 65,300,000 tons, oil at 148 million tons, and other outputs in heavy industry at comparably increased levels.

These and other figures indicate that the Soviet industrial economy in recent years is expanding, as we have been told a good many times now, at double the rate or somewhat more than double the rate of the American economy, even though our total output of goods and services, however you try to measure it, is still more than double that of the Soviet economy. In most fields of endeavor America is still far ahead as the leading industrial country of a world in which the Soviet Union has become the second leading industrial country. In a few fields the Soviet Union has already surpassed the United States, for example in missiles and in the weight of satellites or spaceships which Soviet scientists and engineers are able to orbit into the extra-terrestrial void. During the last three months of 1960 the Soviet economy produced more steel than the American economy, but this was only because the American steel industry was operating at 50 per cent of capacity with large-scale unemployment, whereas the Soviet steel industry always operates at full capacity and with no unemployment.

It is nonetheless still the case that the Soviet economy is a poor economy compared to that of the United States, even though it is a rich economy compared to that of most of Asia, Africa, and Latin America. Russian living standards have risen markedly in recent years, but in consumer goods the Soviet Union is still far behind the United States, both in terms of the quantities of such goods produced, to say nothing of quality, and in terms of relatively high prices, including the turnover tax, in relationship to wages, salaries, and purchasing power. Even during a business recession the United States produces about 5,000,000 cars per year; the Soviet Union still produces less than 200,000 passenger cars per year. Russia produced 1,000,000 washing machines in 1960; America produced more than 3,500,000. Russia produced 500,000 refrigerators in 1960; America produced 3,500,000. Russia produced 1,700,000 television sets in 1960; America produced 5,700,000; and so on.

Now as for sample wages and salaries and some sample prices of goods in stores—and these are all the same throughout the entire expanse of the Soviet Union—let me put the figures in the new rubles introduced in January of 1961, each of which is worth ten of the old rubles and has a theoretical value of $1.10. We shall not go seriously wrong if we think of the new ruble as roughly equal to one dollar. Monthly wages of unskilled workers average by now, I should think, about 50 rubles and of skilled workers 80 rubles. Physicians, a relatively unprivileged group in Russia—three-quarters of them are women—earn from 80 to 150 rubles a month; a few somewhat more. The pilots of Aeroflot, the Soviet civil air service, earn 380 rubles a month; the hostesses on planes about 120 rubles a month. Army marshals, cabinet ministers, and industrial managers earn 500 rubles a month or more, many of the industrial managers considerably more in the form of bonuses and prizes. Popular novelists, actors, actresses, ballerinas, and musicians may earn as much as 3,000 or 4,000 rubles a month.

Let us note a few prices. Most cigarettes are 40 kopeks a pack; beer 50 kopeks or ½ ruble a bottle; women's hose (*Kapron*) 1½ to 2½ rubles; simple women's dresses 30 rubles; theater and opera tickets 1 to 3 rubles; ready-made men's suits 100 to

160 rubles; small cameras 40 to 90 rubles; television sets 200 rubles and up; bicycles 60 to 80 rubles; motorcycles 700 rubles, etc. All prices include the turnover tax, which was long the chief source of public revenue and capital accumulation.

We are in the presence then not of an affluent society of high wages and low prices but of a still poor society of low wages and high prices, even though this society grows less poor each year. In viewing Soviet living standards let us not exaggerate Soviet poverty but take into full account a number of very important facts which are not reflected in wages and prices. Most Soviet workers are on a forty-hour week. All Soviet workers get two to four weeks vacation with full pay each year. All Soviet workers enjoy the benefits of a comprehensive system of social insurance. Few Soviet citizens are troubled with unemployment. Few Soviet families pay more than 5 per cent of family income for rent, including most household services, because the huge Soviet residential housing industry is operated more as a public service than as a business enterprise. All dental service is free; all medical service is free; all hospital care is free; all education is free, with university students paid living stipends. All these things mean that Soviet living standards, even for the poorest of the poor, are considerably higher than wages and prices would suggest.

Is this an egalitarian society? Is this a classless society? The answer to both of these questions is "no." Inequality of incomes is probably greater than inequality of wages and salaries in the United States, although not, of course, greater than inequalities of all incomes in the United States, including incomes derived from ownership of property. In the Soviet economy there are no incomes derived from private ownership of property, whether real estate or industrial property or corporate stocks or bonds. There are no oil millionaires and there is no stock market, but it is a fact that, in terms of wages and salaries, inequalities in the Soviet economy are on the whole greater than they are in the United States.

And of course there are still classes, very definite and fairly readily defined classes. There is a privileged and well-to-do managerial and intellectual elite. There is a large and growing and relatively prosperous "middle class," and there are two less privileged and less prosperous lower classes, namely urban industrial workers and rural collective farmers. In view of widespread misconceptions in the West it might be well to emphasize that neither Marx nor Engels nor Lenin nor Stalin nor Khrushchev ever advocated equality of incomes during the period of socialism nor ever contended that the socialist society would be, or could be, a "classless society." All insisted that there must be inequality of incomes in a socialist society, since in Marxist vocabulary the distributive principle of socialism is: "From each according to his ability, to each according to his work." All insisted further that under socialism there would still be distinctive social classes, but there would be no antagonistic or hostile social classes.

There is some validity in this view in contemporary Soviet society, and this for a fairly obvious reason. Soviet society is a flourishing and rapidly growing society with an annual rate of economic expansion of 7 to 9 per cent of Gross National Product. This makes for great social mobility and for a constant process whereby many scores of thousands of people, by working hard, by becoming educated, by acquiring new skills, rise rapidly from the lower income groups to higher income groups, from the lower classes to the middle classes, and from the middle classes to the ranks of the managerial and intellectual elite. And this process will surely go on so long as the Soviet economy continues to expand at its present rate.

What of the more remote future? The ultimate

millennial ideal of the Marxists is a final transition
from socialism to economic communism, when the
distributive principle will be: "From each according to his ability; to each according to his needs."
Then and only then, according to the Marxist gospel, will there be a truly classless society, and then
and only then will there take place the "withering
away of the State." The State will wither away, say
the Marxists, because the State is always an instru-
mentality of class rule, and in a classless society
there will be no class rule and therefore no State. If
we ask whether this formulation, this aspiration,
this prophecy, as reflected in Program III of the
CPSU as adopted at Party Congress XXII in October, 1961, makes any sense in terms of the probable
future of Soviet society, our best answer, I believe,
is that this vision cannot and will not be realized
in Marx's terms in any future that can now be fore-
seen. Soviet society will never be classless, and the
Soviet State, which is still a totalitarian State although no longer a police-state, is wholly unlikely
to wither away.

But in pursuit of this curious vision some interesting developments are likely to take place, when
Soviet society attains a level of prosperity at which
there will be a superabundance of all goods and

services. At this point, I should guess, all housing will be free, as all education and all medical services are already free. At this point, or before this point, most or all direct taxes will be abolished. The Soviet income tax, which has never been higher than 13 per cent, is scheduled to disappear, by gradual stages, by 1965. Ultimately it may be that all direct and personal taxation as we ordinarily understand and experience taxation will disappear, although the regressive "turnover tax" will long go on. And ultimately it may be that certain elementary necessities of life, beginning with bread, may become free goods, with other goods step by step being made available to consumers without payment of a price. Whether all of this will be a good thing or a bad thing, a blessing or a curse, I am sure I do not know. But it will be something new under the sun.

The further future beyond these quite possible and even probable developments is shrouded in the mysteries of things to come. Meanwhile in the shorter run, which may prove very long, the imperatives and the problems of mass industrialization, mass urbanization, and mass education are, believe it or not, making Soviet society and American society more and more alike, despite their wholly different origins and their wholly different and presumably antithetical ideologies, institutions, aspirations, and long established patterns for the management of human affairs. The noted Frenchman, Alexis de Tocqueville, who published his great work *Democracy in America* in 1839, over a century ago, wrote that Russia and America, "starting from different points, tend toward the same end." His prediction is being realized in our time, although in a fashion quite different from what he envisaged.

Our customary stereotypes lead us to suppose that America means freedom, that Russia means slavery; that America means democracy, that Russia means dictatorship; that America means private business enterprise and that Russia means socialism; that America means respect for the dignity of the individual and that Russia makes the individual a tool of the State, etc. These dichotomies all have validity on a certain level of distinction. But rather more meaningful in terms of the daily and yearly lives of human beings is the inevitable and unplanned process, which the anthropologists like to call "cultural convergence," whereby wholly different societies become more and more alike by virtue of the influence upon them of vast impersonal trends and forces which may have been set in motion for wholly different reasons or motives but which prove to be strikingly similar in their impact on human lives.

Russia and America alike in our time are societies of Big Cities with similar problems of urban planning, slum clearance, traffic jams, and suburban commuters. Russia and America alike in our time are societies of Big Business with comparable problems of industrial management and public control. Russia and America in our time are societies of Big Labor with comparable problems of the relations between management and labor, despite the absence of collective bargaining and strikes in the Soviet Union, and with comparable problems of the relationship of both management and labor to the public, whose voice of course in Russia is that of the Communist Party. Russia and America alike in our time are societies of Big Agriculture, even though Soviet farming wastes far more labor and is still far less productive than American farming. Between the two societies there are, to be sure, major divergencies. But the similarities and convergences far outweigh the differences.

Are we worried about juvenile delinquency? So are the Russians. Are we concerned with rising rates of crime and divorce? So are the Russians.

Are we anxious about graft and influence and shady deals in Big Business, Big Labor, and Big Government? So are the Russians. Are we unhappy about the pressures which all too often make executives, and many other people as well, victims of stomach ulcers, hypertension, alcoholism, neuroses, psychoses, and sometimes suicide? So are the Russians. The list of common community problems could be almost indefinitely extended. The Russian Communists like to believe that these experiences and problems in America are products of decadent capitalism. Some of us like to believe that these experiences and problems in Russia are products of Communist tyranny. Both are wrong. These problems and experiences are products of mass education, mass industrialization, and mass urbanization—and it makes little difference to most people whether these inexorable and inevitable processes of community growth, and of what we used to call "progress," go on within a framework of socialism or a framework of capitalism.

If we and the Russians have similar problems and anxieties in our time, we also have similar aspirations and similar tasks of building a productive and prosperous society in which individual freedom—hitherto maximized in America and minimized in Russia—can be reconciled with community welfare—hitherto minimized in America and maximized in Russia. We do in truth move toward the same end. We may rejoice that this is so, for we are all together, whether we know it or not, common citizens of One World and all together members of humankind, who can learn much from one another and teach much to one another, provided that we are not so stupid and devilish as to destroy one another, and possibly most of the human race, in a thermonuclear Third World War.

We are also engaged, whether we know it or not, in common tasks of human amelioration and human salvation so that posterity may have a human future. And in these tasks we are still guided, as we should be, by the laws and the prophets of ancient days. Despite the Cold War we and the Russians are unwittingly engaged, and will on the horizons of tomorrow be knowingly engaged, in fruitful competition and co-operation in the common task of mankind—to preserve and enrich the human heritage and to promote some sense of the common citizenship of all men and women everywhere in the world. So long as we can believe that this is in any sense so, we have no need to despair of the future.

Lecture Three

Beyond the Cold War

SOME TWENTY-FIVE HUNDRED YEARS AGO AN AN-
cient Greek poet named Hesiod composed a series
of verses which have survived and come down to
us under the title of *The Works and Days*. Among
these verses is one which reads in part as follows in
Richmond Lattimore's recent translation:

It was never true that there was only one kind of strife. There have always been two on earth. There is one you could like when you understand her. The other is hateful. The two strifes have separate natures. There is one strife who builds up evil war and slaughter. She is harsh. No man loves her. But under compulsion and by will of the immortals, men promote this rough strife. But the other one was born the elder daughter of black night. The son of Kronos who sits on high and dwells in the bright air set her in the roots of the earth and among men. She is far kinder. She pushes the shiftless man to work for all his laziness. A man looks at his neighbor who is rich; then he too wants work. For the rich man presses on with his plowing and planting and the ordering of his state. So the neighbor envies the neighbor who presses on toward wealth. Such strife is a good friend to mortals.

The crucial question of our time, the question upon which depends the good fortune or the misfortune of the human race and quite possibly its survival or suicide, is that of whether the global strife between America and Russia must take or will take the evil form of war and slaughter or may take the form, if we and the rulers of Russia so will it and can come to terms, of a constructive, creative competition in the works of peace. Rivalry in the works of peace is a good friend to mortals, since everyone gains and no one loses in a competition to see which contestant can achieve more and contribute more toward the goal of a good life in a good society. Rivalry in the works of war can have no other ultimate result than the mutual ruination and coannihilation of the contestants.

Only a prophet with powers of prediction far beyond those which any of us here can claim would venture to forecast which form of strife will come ultimately to prevail between Russia and America. All of us in America and Russia alike who are not intolerant fanatics, and who are not hypnotized by what Sigmund Freud called "the death instinct," hope and pray that the inevitable and unending strife between Russia and America will be creative and not destructive. Whether in fact this will be so, we do not know. But we can explore the nature of the problem and the shape of the alternatives which loom ahead in the hope that a reasoned and reasonable exploration may contribute to creative strife rather than to destructive strife. Therefore let us explore the problem without prejudice as to its most probable outcome.

We live in a time of crisis and thus of ever recurring crises in East-West relations and world affairs. I am told that in the Mandarin language of China the idiographic sign for "crisis" consists of two symbols, one of which alone means "danger" and the other of which alone means "opportunity." Let us consider at the outset the nature of the dangers and the opportunities of our time of crisis, with the aid of some quotations from some of the responsible participants, before we consider the problem of the origins and course and possible outcome of the Cold War.

The danger we face is clear, or ought to be clear, to those of us still capable of constructive cerebration. The danger is not Communism *per se*, although many among us quite honestly and sincerely believe that Communism is our greatest danger. Our greatest danger, as I see it, is not the Communist challenge as such; it is a continuation and extension of international anarchy, of power politics, of war—all of which are age-old habits of mankind—into the thermonuclear age when persistence in such habits may well spell the end of the human species.

More specifically, if we do not soon negotiate an end of the arms race as a step toward negotiating an end of the Cold War, we shall face the danger, if indeed we have not already reached this point, where effective control of our destinies will pass out of our hands, and out of the hands of our political leaders, into the hands of professional military people and of the munitions industry. This danger is greater in America than in Russia, for Russia has no privately owned munitions industry operated for private profit. And in Russia the Army is fully controlled by the Party, as Marshal Zhukov discovered in 1957. This danger in America was put as follows by President Eisenhower in his farewell address of January 17, 1961: "We must guard against the acquisition of unwarranted influence, whether sought or unsought, by the military-industrial complex. The potential rise of misplaced power exists and will persist."

In the second place, if we do not soon negotiate an end of the arms race, we shall face the ever mounting danger of "accidental" war touched off by nervous bomber pilots, anxious technicians at missile bases, or neurotic scanners of radar screens. Policy-making is already passing out of the hands of policy-makers into the hands of the button-pushers. In the era of Intercontinental Ballistic Missiles warning time of a real or imagined enemy attack is reduced to fifteen minutes, which means that there can be no national policy-making by national policy-makers. The sword of Damocles was a very mild menace indeed compared to the danger already with us, day and night, of a thermonuclear holocaust precipitated by mistake.

In the third place, if we do not soon negotiate an end to the arms race, we shall soon face the prospect of more and more nations joining the thermonuclear suicide club and of more and more stockpiles of infernal weapons bringing mankind ever closer to self-destruction. If we are wise, I believe we must heed the words of C. P. Snow, the distinguished British scientist and novelist, speaking to fellow-scientists in New York on December 27, 1960:

> We genuinely know the risks. We are faced with an either/or and we haven't much time. Either—we accept a restriction on nuclear armaments. This is going to begin just as a token with an agreement on the stopping of nuclear tests. The United States is not going to get the 99 per cent security that it has been asking for. It is unobtainable, though there are other bargains that the United States could probably secure. I am not going to conceal from you that this course involves certain risks. They are quite obvious and no honest man is going to blink them. That is the "either."

The "or" is not a risk but a certainty. It is this. There is no agreement on tests. The nuclear arms race between the USA and the USSR not only continues but accelerates. Other countries join in. Within at the most six years China and several other States have a stock of nuclear bombs. Within at the most ten years, some of these bombs are going off. I am saying this as responsibly as I can. That is the certainty. On the one side, therefore, we have a finite risk. On the other side we have a certainty of disaster. Between a risk and a certainty, a sane man does not hesitate. It is the plain duty of scientists to explain this either/or. It is a duty which seems to me to come from the moral nature of scientific activity itself.

As for the opportunities looming before us, they are many and exciting, but I limit them for the moment to the recent hopeful words of Premier Nikita Khrushchev and President John Kennedy. In his telegram congratulating Kennedy on his election, Khrushchev declared: "We are ready to develop the most friendly relations between the Soviet and the American peoples, between the governments of the USSR and the USA. We are convinced that there are no insurmountable obstacles to the preservation and consolidation of peace."

In his Inaugural Address Kennedy asserted, "Let us begin anew, remembering on both sides that civility is not a sign of weakness, and sincerity is always subject to proof. Let us negotiate not out of fear, but let us not fear to negotiate." And in his State of the Union message Kennedy called for "open and peaceful competition for prestige, for markets, for scientific achievements, even for men's minds. I have already taken steps to make arms control a central goal of our national policy under my direction. I now invite all nations including the Soviet Union to join with us in developing a weather prediction program, in a new communications satellite program, and in preparations for probing the distant planets of Mars and Venus, probes which may someday unlock the deepest secrets of the universe."

The Kennedy Administration has recruited some of the best minds in America and is busily engaged in a fundamental re-examination of the Cold War, of foreign policy in all its aspects, of defense policy and armament policy and disarmament policy and of many other matters. All of this surely is to be warmly welcomed, and it is to be hoped that this bold enterprise in exploring new frontiers will challenge the power-holders and the policy-makers of the Soviet

Union to a comparable re-examination of policies and purposes, of ends and means, of dangers and opportunities, so that the energies of mankind in the One World of our time may be progressively diverted from preparations for universal death to competitive and co-operative endeavors in the service of the good life.

It would be altogether inappropriate and futile at this time for any of us or all of us to try to anticipate or evaluate the results of the Kennedy re-examination and, I hope, of the Khrushchev re-examination of where we have been, where we are, and where we wish to go. Judgment must wait on conclusions and policies which are still to be formulated during the weeks and months which lie ahead. Meanwhile it is fitting and proper, and I trust peculiarly useful at this crucial turning point in human fortunes, to look at the record and to see what tentative conclusions may be drawn. The time is overripe for reassessing the origins and courses and lessons of the Cold War—the lessons already learned and the lessons still to be learned.

It is a somewhat curious fact that, although many books have been written on various aspects of the Cold War, no book had been published prior to 1961 dealing with the struggle as a whole, with two exceptions. A British newsman, Kenneth Ingram, published in 1955 a short journalistic volume entitled *A History of the Cold War*. An American professor, John Lucaks, published in 1960 another short *History of the Cold War*. Both of these are sketchy commentaries, although useful and thought-provoking. Fortunately, Professor Denna Frank Fleming, Professor Emeritus of Vanderbilt University, has given a detailed and documented account of the whole matter (thus far neglected, to the loss and peril of us all, because of the "unpopularity" of its interpretations and conclusions in an America hypnotized by its anti-Communist syndrome): *The Cold War and Its Origins*, Volume I, 1917–1950, Volume II, 1950–1960, 1168 pages (London: George Allen and Unwin, Spring, 1961; New York: Doubleday, Autumn, 1961). This will long remain the "definitive" account of the Cold War and the most eloquent plea for its nonviolent resolution.

At all events, what we have long been calling the "Cold War" did not begin in 1945, in the aftermath of World War II and of the Yalta and Potsdam conferences. In a broader sense it began with the second Russian Revolution of 1917. The Communists were then convinced that the Russian Revolution would inevitably be followed by worldwide revolution and that it was their mission and duty to assist the inevitable to come to pass. The non-Communists and anti-Communists of the West were then convinced that the Communist regime in Russia would inevitably collapse and that it was their duty and mission to assist the inevitable to come to pass. Both sides, along with almost all other statesmen and peoples, shared what Norman Angell in 1910 called "The Great Illusion"—namely, the belief that national interests can be rationally served by war. Furthermore, Communists then believed Communism could be extended by war, and anti-Communists believed that Communism could be destroyed by war. Both were wrong.

Within ten months after Russia's October Revolution, Soviet Russia and the West were at war. And the war was not a cold war but a hot war, marked by many casualties and vast destruction. Be it remembered, lest we forget what Russians never forget, that this war was not begun by Communists sending armies against the West but by the West sending armies against Soviet Russia. In 1918 and 1919 American troops killed Russians and were killed by Russians on Russian soil, along with British troops and French troops and Japanese troops and Polish troops and a good many others in another somber chapter of Russia's age-old tragedy of invasion from abroad. The legacy of mutual fear and suspicion and hatred which nourished the Cold War of the 1940's and '50's originated in the hot war between East and West in 1918–1921. The outcome of this war was a deadlock or stalemate. The United States and the Allied Powers failed to destroy the Soviet regime and were obliged to abandon their armed intervention and blockade. The Communist rulers of Russia failed to undermine or subvert any of the Capitalist States and were obliged to give up or defer their hopes of World Revolution.

Problems of power in international politics can be dealt with in one of two ways—either by violence, in which each side seeks to impose its will upon, or to destroy, the other side by armed force; or by bargaining, in which both sides compromise their differences or agree to disagree within a framework of a negotiated *modus vivendi*. The first of these ways is the way of war; the second, the way of diplomacy. When war or preparation for war eventuates in a deadlock or stalemate in which it is evident to all that neither side can impose its will on the other or destroy the other, or that both will be destroyed in the event of a resort to force, then only one other way is left for dealing with problems of power among the Great Powers of our world—i.e., the way of diplomacy, an ancient and honorable art which, when wisely practiced, is the art of maintaining peace among rival sovereignties in a State System lacking world government. These are simple truisms and self-evident statements of the obvious. But for forty years and more many Americans have been reluctant to understand or act upon these eternal verities of international relations. And at times, although far less consistently, Russian policy-makers, particularly in the last years of Stalin's autocracy, have been equally obtuse.

Take note, if you will, of two simple and obvious corollaries of the truisms just mentioned. The first is that in order to practice diplomacy, it is necessary to have diplomatic relations with those with whom you expect to practice diplomacy. Otherwise, obviously, no diplomacy is possible. Russians have always known this. Americans have great difficulty in getting this through their heads, as shown by American refusal for sixteen years to enter into diplomatic relations with Soviet Russia and by American refusal in our time to enter into diplomatic relations with Communist China or North Korea or North Vietnam or East Germany. The second corollary is that in the practice of diplomacy one cannot, if one hopes for agreement, always say "no" or "nyet" to all the proposals and suggestions of the other side. One must sometimes say "perhaps" and one must occasionally say "yes." This, too, Americans sometimes do not understand and Russians sometimes do not understand.

Back in the early 1920's all of these things were quite well understood and acted upon in the Soviet Russia of Lenin, Chicherin, and Litvinov, and in most of the major countries of the world, with the exception of the United States. The result was the establishment of diplomatic relations, the practice of diplomacy, the negotiation of a *modus vivendi* or pattern of coexistence between Russia and the West. This pattern of coexistence endured to the mutual advantage of all concerned for almost twenty years, with no Cold War and with no violence or threats of violence. I believe this pattern unquestionably would have continued indefinitely, even down to the present day, except for the circumstance that, under the impact of the Great Depression of the early 1930's (which Marxists mistakenly assumed was a vindication of the Marxist analysis of capitalism), millions of Germans and Japanese found their souls by losing their minds and collectively embarked under the leadership of madmen upon national programs of mass murder and mass suicide.

Cold War as we have known it for the past dozen years and more had its genesis, believe it or not, in the divergent responses of the Soviet Union and the Western democracies to the common challenge of Fascism in the 1930's. Bear with me in a bit of power politics analysis, and I am sure you will agree that this in fact was the case.

Suppose we proceed backward in time by way of establishing causal relationships among crucial events and decisions in world affairs. The Cold War in the narrower sense began in the late summer and fall of 1945, immediately after the surrender of Japan, with early, repeated, and emphatic American and British protests against the imposition of Soviet hegemony and Communist power on Eastern Europe north of Greece and east of the Elbe and the Adriatic. This vast and alarming extension of Russian power into Central Europe and the Balkans was alleged in London and Washington to constitute a Russian violation of the Yalta and Potsdam agreements of 1945, although it might perhaps be better said that it was a violation of the Anglo-American interpretation of these highly ambiguous and imprecise agreements, not necessarily a violation of the Soviet interpretation of the agreements. This expansion of Soviet power was also alleged to constitute a new totalitarian enslavement of the peoples of Eastern Europe, who must somehow be "liberated" and given the blessings of Western democracy, even though most of them had never known any of those blessings before.

How and why did this condition of affairs come about? It came about because Hitler and his psychopathic colleagues and followers, having conquered Western Europe and having failed to conquer Britain, decided in 1940–1941 to attempt the conquest of Russia. It came about because the Russians finally defeated the Nazi *Wehrmacht* before Moscow in 1941 and at Stalingrad in 1942–1943 at an utterly appalling cost in life and property, representing at least ten times the casualties and material losses suffered in World War II by all the other United Nations combined. (It came about because Russian armies fought their way westward to Berlin and Prague and Vienna and the Adriatic before Anglo-American armies were able to fight their way from the Channel to Eastern Europe.) It came about because America and Britain were unable to establish any effective second front against Hitler's Reich, despite the North African and Italian campaigns, until the Normandy invasion of June, 1944, with the Russians meanwhile bearing almost the entire burden of the war.

And why were the Western Powers, until the last few months of a six-year war, unable to contribute more effectively to Hitler's defeat and to occupy more of Europe before the Russians occupied it? The answer surely lies in the "Peace" of Munich of September, 1938, whereby the Western Powers betrayed Czechoslovakia and in effect gave Hitler a free hand in Eastern Europe and the Balkans in the rather obvious hope that he would attack Russia and leave the Western Powers at peace. The meaning of Munich, as a few of us pointed out at the time, was that the Western democracies, in a mistaken quest for peace, were surrendering Eastern Europe and that Eastern Europe would therefore pass under Nazi control, or be partitioned between Germany and Russia, or possibly pass under Russian control if Hitler's efforts to conquer Russia and the world should finally fail. All of these things came to pass in succession. The Western Powers did not surrender Eastern Europe at Potsdam or Yalta or on the bloody beachheads of Normandy in 1944. They surrendered Eastern Europe at Munich in 1938.

In international politics, as in our personal affairs,

decisions have consequences. These consequences are often irrevocable. The consequences of Munich were irrevocable. They are with us today. They will be with us for a long time to come. The Cold War originated in Russian determination, thus far successful, to capitalize on the consequences and in Western determination, thus far unsuccessful, to undo or reverse these consequences. The matter is as simple as that.

If the Cold War is now possibly approaching an end, this is because policy-makers in West and East alike are now disposed to accept the consequences of power politics over the last twenty years or more, since the risks of not accepting them are far greater than the risks of accepting them. No good purpose is served for the present or future by rehashing the mistakes and crimes of the past on either side. Suffice it to say that the pattern of power implicit in the Cold War, and indeed the source of the Cold War, emerged from the agonies and tragedies and long belated triumphs which followed the decisions of the Fascist leaders in 1941 to attack Russia in June and to attack America in December of that fateful year. The ultimate result was to bring Russian power to the Elbe and the Adriatic. The Cold War is a product of the fears and suspicions and mutual doubts and mistrusts generated among the major members of the United Nations coalition in the wake of the almost ineluctable consequences of the "Peace" of Munich and of the ensuing global strategy of World War II.

By the spring of 1953 it had become obvious to some of us who try to study these matters with care that the Cold War had become a totally senseless and highly dangerous conflict which had to be ended by negotiated accords among the Great Powers, meaning in the first instance the United States and the Soviet Union as the greatest of the Powers. This conviction was reinforced by the removal from this vale of tears in March of 1953 of Joseph Stalin and his temporary deposit on his bed of repose next to Lenin in the tomb on Red Square. It is clear from the record that Stalin in his later years had become a psychopathic victim of paranoia, with whom no meaningful diplomatic negotiations outside of Russia were possible and no meaningful human relations inside of Russia were possible. A new leadership in the Soviet Union offered new possibilities. By the spring of 1953, and years before the advent of the ICBM and the Sputniks and the Luniks, it was already abundantly clear that neither America nor Russia could impose its will upon the other by armed force and that any effort so to do could result only in mutual

destruction. Therefore, to revert to the obvious truisms with which we began, it was clear by 1953 that
there was no tolerable alternative to a revival of diplomacy and a negotiated settlement of the Cold
War.

In the June 20, 1953, issue of *The Nation*, a pro-
phetic article appeared, entitled "Cold War's End."
It forecast peace in Korea, peace in Indochina, a
treaty for a neutralized Austria, a summit conference,
an ultimate solution of the German problem, and
much else, all of which could have come to pass and
should have come to pass within two or three years
after 1953. Some of these things did materialize, but
not all.

A truce in Korea was signed in June, 1953. A
truce in Indochina was signed in July, 1954. An
Austrian treaty was signed on May 15, 1955. A summit conference met in Geneva in July, 1955, and
there was every prospect for a negotiated settlement of the Cold War by the end of that year.
Then something went wrong, and the Cold War
was resumed.

What went wrong in 1955? Well, many things,
various things, including major miscalculations by
policy-makers in both Washington and Moscow,
and also in London and Paris and Budapest and

Cairo and elsewhere. Among other things, President Eisenhower's heart attack of September, 1955, left him temporarily incapacitated and left the direction of American policy in the hands of a Secretary of State who, amid his many virtues, was addicted to the vice of opposing any negotiated settlement of the Cold War. If a comprehensive East-West settlement had been negotiated in 1955, the tragedies on the Danube and on the Nile in the fall of 1956 might have been averted.

It is later than you think; 1961–1962 is a good deal later than 1955, but happily not too late. Unless further major mistakes and miscalculations are made, the Cold War can well be ended by a series of diplomatic settlements during the coming year and thereafter. There was, of course, a possibility of negotiating an end of the arms race and the Cold War in 1959 or 1960. This opportunity was wasted, partly because of Russian and American persistence in adhering to the outworn patterns of the past. We blame the Russians; the Russians blame us. This is human nature. No good ever comes from such exercises in condemnation and self-righteousness.

The facts are clear enough. American-Soviet negotiations over the German problem led to the unsuccessful Geneva Conference of Foreign Ministers between May and August of 1959. This led to President Eisenhower's invitation to Khrushchev to tour America, which he did in September of 1959. This in turn led to further agreement that a summit conference should meet in Paris in May of 1960, to be followed by Eisenhower's tour of the Soviet Union. Much good might have come of these arrangements. All was lost with the summit fiasco in Paris of May, 1960.

Yet certain conclusions flow from that fiasco. Among the conclusions are these: the practice of diplomacy on any level is not possible unless all the parties abide by the rules of international law and diplomatic practice which the nations have agreed on through the centuries; further, governments engaged in diplomacy must never tell lies in public if there is the slightest possibility that another government may have proof that your lie is a lie; further, governments and chiefs of state must never acknowledge official responsibility for espionage agents who have been exposed and arrested by some other government; further, governments always express regrets and tender apologies to other governments when they are caught in a flagrant violation of international law; and finally, no useful diplomatic relations are ever possible with the head of a govern-

ment who does not know what his own subordinates
are doing and who is not master of his household.

The larger and far more fateful issues confront-
ing us amount to this: What changes in established Russian attitudes and policies would seem to
be called for if the Soviet Union is to make its necessary contribution to peace? And what changes in
established American attitudes and policies would
seem to be called for if the United States is to make
its necessary contribution to peace? I approach this
problem with diffidence and humility by virtue of
acute awareness that, for many years and even decades, Americans have been telling Russians what to
do and what not to do, while Russians have been telling Americans what to do and what not to do. On this
point I quote Dr. Brock Chisholm, the famous Cana-
dian psychiatrist, formerly with the United Nations
Health Organization and erstwhile director of the
World Association for Mental Health. In a little book
entitled *Prescription for Survival* (1957), Dr. Chisholm wrote as follows:

> Very frequently one hears the United Nations
> criticized as a debating society. That's pri-
> marily what it is for. It is there to provide an
> opportunity for governments to talk out the
> world's problems. Many people might accept
> the idea of the debating society, but interpret

it to mean that the United Nations is a place
where we go to reproach other people for being the way they are. This is an old, old habit.
Man's method of dealing with difficulty in the
past has always been to tell everyone else how
they should behave. We've all been doing that
for centuries. It should be clear by now that
this no longer does any good. Everybody has
by now been told by everybody else how he
should behave. Therefore, everybody knows
how everybody else thinks he should behave.
The criticism is not effective; it never has been
and it is never going to be. There is only one
telling that is effective—our telling ourselves
how to behave.

Let us hope, as we try to tell ourselves how to behave, that the Russians are also trying to tell themselves how to behave. The rulers of Russia, I believe,
have learned, whether they choose to admit the fact
or not, that the Marxist analysis of capitalism is simply wrong and has no basis whatever in the realities
of our time, particularly in the United States of
America. They have also learned, I believe, that
Communism will never liberate or subjugate or unify
all the world and that Communism's future fortunes
in the world cannot be served by propaganda or by
subversion or by revolution and least of all by war,

but can be served only by demonstrating that the Communist system in the long run may be able to contribute more effectively than other systems to human health, wealth, and happiness, and ultimately to human freedom. The policy-makers and most of the people in America, in my judgment, have by now learned (despite the aberrations of 1961) that war as a weapon of national policy has become wholly unthinkable, intolerable, and impossible, and that peace requires that America and Russia deal with one another as equals, with interests and aspirations which are quite compatible. Beyond this point, much more needs to be learned by Russians and Americans alike, including the ultimate lesson that enduring peace in the world community requires effective law in the world community and that this will finally require agreement on some limited and workable form of world government.

But apart from this ultimate lesson, there are several other lessons closer at hand which I believe will have to be learned and I hope are in process of being learned. One of these lessons is that "neutralism" or a policy of nonalignment on the part of other nations is not immoral, as Secretary John Foster Dulles repeatedly said, but is highly desirable as a contribution to peace, and that the neutralization of certain areas by international agreement is also highly desirable as a contribution to peace. Russia and America have entered into some such agreements. More are called for. The Austrian Treaty of 1955 restored the independence of Austria as a neutralist and unaligned state and provided for the disengagement and withdrawal of Russian and Western troops from Austria. British Prime Minister Anthony Eden at the summit conference in Geneva in July, 1955, urged a program of disengagement, denuclearization, demilitarization, and neutralization in Central Europe. Polish Foreign Minister Adam Rapacki, taking up this British idea, urged a similar plan in 1957. It was endorsed by the Russians but rejected, I believe unwisely, by Washington. In December, 1959, however, twelve nations including America and Russia, very sagaciously signed a treaty for the denuclearization, demilitarization, and neutralization of the continent of Antarctica. Both America and Russia have ratified this treaty, which could become and should become the model for another treaty denuclearizing, demilitarizing, and neutralizing outer space.

It is above all imperative that both America and Russia should respect the neutralism of unaligned or neutralized States. The current crisis over Laos illustrates the dangers of not respecting neutralism. President Kennedy is appealing to the Russians to respect the neutralism of Laos and has warned that the Western Powers cannot permit Laos, which is geographically a perfect buffer State between the two great coalitions, to be taken over by Communists or pro-Communists. In this he is quite right, and he is also wise and right in not coupling the warning with any threats or denunciations. The present crisis would not have arisen had American policy-makers during the Eisenhower Administration been willing to grant *quid pro quo* that the Communist Powers also cannot permit Laos to be taken over by anti-Communists seeking to align Laos with the Western Powers against Russia and China and North Vietnam. This American policy-makers were unwilling to do.

At the Geneva conference of 1954 which ended the Indochinese war, it was clearly understood that the newly independent kingdoms of Cambodia and Laos were to be neutralist. Chou En Lai, Premier of Red China, appealed to the United States to join in an international guarantee of the neutral status of Cambodia and Laos. Secretary Dulles refused. He also refused to make the United States a signatory of the Geneva agreements, but he promised that the United States would respect those agreements. I fear the record will show that this promise was not kept. Washington at once sent a military mission to Laos, even though dressed in civilian clothes. Washington immediately began recruiting, feeding, clothing, and arming the Laotian Army on which over three hundred million dollars of American money have been spent since 1954. Washington persuaded the government of Laos in 1958 to dismiss the control commission consisting of representatives from Canada, India, and Poland, which had been established at the Geneva conference to assure the neutralism of Laos. And when truly neutralist Premier Souvanna Phouma was restored to power in August, 1960, Washington gave its support to pro-Western and bitterly anti-Communist General Phoumi Nosovan, who in December, 1960, with Washington's blessing, overthrew Premier Phouma and replaced him with pro-American puppet, Prince Boun Oum.

Washington, in short, violated the neutralist status of Laos and invited counter-violation by North Vietnam and the Soviet Union. The Kennedy Administration has since declared that it wants a truly neutral Laos and has proposed a restoration of the control commission and a new international conference, if need be, to assure the neutral status of Laos. We must hope that the men of Moscow will accept these assurances and proposals in good faith and that the crisis over Laos and the civil war in Laos will be terminated by a true return to neutralism. Meanwhile, Washington policy-makers have involved themselves in support of a corrupt and discredited regime in South Vietnam (1961–1962), thus inviting further failure or disaster.

There are a few other broad lessons that need to be learned here. I think we shall need to learn, firstly, that no unification of Germany is possible except on the basis of some form of disengagement, disarmament, and neutralization. I think we shall need to learn, secondly, that no liberation nor relaxation of Communist control over the satellite States of Eastern Europe is possible without some form of disengagement, disarmament, and neutralization. I suspect we shall need to learn, thirdly, that no progress in disarmament is possible through dramatic Soviet schemes for abolishing all armed forces and weapons in four years or so, or through American insistence on 100 per cent foolproof schemes of inspection and control, all of which are technological and political impossibilities. Agreements to reduce armaments require good faith, and they require also a negotiated settlement of political problems through the practice of diplomacy as a means of diminishing mutual fears and suspicions and contributing toward mutual confidence.

Fourthly, I think we shall need to learn that we here in America will in fact need in the years ahead a large-scale economic substitute for the Cold War and the arms race. A Kennedy task force is working on this now. No task could be more important. And fifthly and finally, and obviously still far off, I think we shall need to learn that no stable and secure world settlement will be truly possible without some form of participation by China, since China embraces one-quarter of the human race with a population far larger than that of America, Russia, and all of Western Europe combined.

Can we learn these lessons? I believe so. We must learn them or perish; therefore we can learn them if we will choose fruitful life rather than universal death for ourselves and our children. Let us help ourselves, let us help our leaders, let us help even our competitors and enemies to learn these lessons. For the more we learn, the more true will become the words of Him whose death and resurrection all Christians over the world celebrate every Easter: "Blessed are the peacemakers, for they shall be called the children of God." And the sooner we learn these lessons, the sooner will dawn the day, as forecast by Isaiah, one of the greatest of the prophets of Israel, when the people "shall beat their swords into plowshares and their spears into pruning hooks, nation shall not lift up sword against nation; neither shall they learn war any more." And finally, the sooner we learn these lessons, the sooner, in the words of Hesiod, will we abandon the strife that builds up evil war and slaughter and embrace the kind of strife and creative rivalry which is a good thing to mortals.

Selected Bibliography

AUBREY, HENRY C. With the assistance of JOEL DARM-
STADTER. *Coexistence: Economic Challenge and Response.* Washington: National Planning Association,
1961.

BAILEY, THOMAS A. *America Faces Russia.* Ithaca,
N. Y.: Cornell Univ. Press, 1951.

BARGHOORN, FREDERICK C. *The Soviet Image of the
United States.* New York: Harcourt, 1950.

BARGHOORN, FREDERICK C. *The Soviet Cultural Offensive.* Princeton, N. J.: Princeton Univ. Press, 1960.

BENTON, WILLIAM. *This Is the Challenge.* New York: Associated College Presses, 1958.

BURNHAM, JAMES. *Containment or Liberation?* New York: Day, 1953.

BYRNES, JAMES. *Speaking Frankly.* New York: Harper, 1947.

DANIELS, ROBERT V. *The Nature of Communism.* New York: Random House, 1962.

DAVISON, W. PHILLIPS. *The Berlin Blockade.* Princeton, N. Y.: Princeton Univ. Press, 1958.

DEAN, VERA MICHELES. *The United States and Russia.* Cambridge: Harvard Univ. Press, 1947.

DENNETT, RAYMOND, and JOHNSON, JOSEPH E. (eds.). *Negotiating With the Russians.* Boston: World Peace Foundation, 1951.

DEUTSCHER, ISAAC. *The Great Contest: Russia and the West.* New York: Oxford Univ. Press, 1960.

DINERSTEIN, H. S. *War and the Soviet Union: Nuclear Weapons and the Revolution in Soviet Military and Political Thinking.* New York: Praeger, 1959.

DRUMMOND, ROSCOE, and COBLENTZ, GASTON. *Duel at the Brink.* Garden City, N. Y.: Doubleday, 1960.

FISCHER, LOUIS. *Russia, America, and the World.* New York: Harper, 1961.

FISHER, HAROLD H. *America and Russia in the World Community.* Claremont, Calif.: Claremont College, 1946.

FLEMING, D. F. *The Cold War and Its Origins.* Vol. I, 1917–1950; Vol. II, 1950–1960. Garden City, N. Y.: Doubleday, 1961.

GAITSKELL, HUGH. *The Challenge of Coexistence.* Cambridge: Harvard Univ. Press, 1957.

GARTHOFF, RAYMOND L. *Soviet Strategy in the Nuclear Age.* New York: Praeger, 1958.

GARTHOFF, RAYMOND L. *The Soviet Image of Future War.* Washington: Public Affairs Press, 1959.

INGRAM, KENNETH. *The History of the Cold War.* New York: Philosophical Library, 1955.

KENNAN, GEORGE F. *Russia, the Atom and the West.* New York: Harper, 1958.

KHRUSHCHEV, NIKITA S. *For Victory in Peaceful Competition With Capitalism.* New York: Dutton, 1960.

KHRUSHCHEV, NIKITA S. *Khrushchev in America.* New York: Crosscurrents Press, 1960.

KHRUSHCHEV, NIKITA S. *Khrushchev in New York* (September–October, 1960). New York: Crosscurrents Press, 1960.

KOVNER, MILTON. *The Challenge of Coexistence.* Washington: Public Affairs Press, 1961.

KULSKI, WLADYSLAW, W. *Peaceful Co-existence: An Analysis of Soviet Foreign Policy.* Chicago: Regnery (in co-operation with Foundation for Foreign Affairs), 1959.

LASERSON, MAX M. *The American Impact on Russia.* New York: Macmillan, 1950.

LIPPMANN, WALTER. *The Communist World and Ours.* Boston: Atlantic-Little, Brown, 1959.

LUKACS, JOHN. *A History of the Cold War.* Garden City, N. Y.: Doubleday, 1961.

MILLS, C. WRIGHT. *The Causes of World War Three.* New York: Simon & Schuster, 1958.

MORRAY, JOSEPH P. *From Yalta to Disarmament.* New York: Monthly Review Press, 1961.

O'CONOR, JOHN F. *Cold War and Liberation.* New York: Vantage Press, 1961.

PERLA, LEO. *Can We End the Cold War?* New York: Macmillan, 1960.

ROBERTS, HENRY L. *Russia and America: Dangers and Prospects.* New York: Harper, 1956.

ROBERTS, LESLIE. *Home From the Cold Wars.* Boston: Beacon Press, 1948.

SETON-WATSON, HUGH. *Neither War Nor Peace.* New York: Praeger, 1960.

STEVENSON, ADLAI E. *Friends and Enemies.* New York: Harper, 1959.

TETENS, T. H. *Germany Plots With the Kremlin.* New York: Schuman, 1953.

U. S. DEPARTMENT OF STATE. *Foreign Ministers Meeting, May–August, 1959, Geneva.* Washington D. C.: Government Printing Office, 1959.

WARBURG, J. P. *How to Co-exist Without Playing the Kremlin's Game.* Boston: Beacon, 1952.

WILLIAMS, W. A. *America-Russian Relations: 1781–1947.* New York: Rinehart, 1952.